PRAISE FOR *ANGELS WE HAVE HEARD ARE HIGH*

"Angels sing and dance in the pages of this book,
awaking readers to God's presence in the ordinary,
tender, and tragic life in which we and others dwell.
The stories, dotted with Charles Schuster's earthy
humor, shine light on pathos and meaning. They
invite us as readers to watch for angels and God
nods in the hurried and often painful moments of
our own lives and the lives of those who touch us."

—MARY ELIZABETH MOORE, DEAN EMERITA
AND PROFESSOR OF THEOLOGY AND EDUCATION,
BOSTON UNIVERSITY SCHOOL OF THEOLOGY

"Charles Schuster's brilliant, unconventional
Christmas book of storytelling treasures proves
not only to be a page-turner, but leaves the reader
gasping for more. Yes, more theological tales
revealing the divine in the ordinary—the phone
call at 1:30 a.m. on Christmas morning, the barking
dog, the squawking baby, the squirrel. With wit and
wisdom, Schuster probes the mysterious universality
of Christmas that transcends Christianity,
prompting others to remember and reminisce, to
imagine and to inspire."

—DONALD E. MESSER, PRESIDENT EMERITUS,
ILIFF SCHOOL OF THEOLOGY

"Vintage Schuster: wry, funny, serious, sometimes all in the same sentence. If you haven't heard of him, though, and have this book in your hands, you're in for a treat. Chuck has an uncanny way of making Christianity accessible and relevant to a contemporary audience. I count it a privilege to know him. After reading his book, you will, too."

—STEPHEN SWECKER, FORMER EDITOR OF *THE PROGRESSIVE CHRISTIAN* MAGAZINE

"When the wit and wisdom of Chuck Schuster meet his pastoral heart, the result is an intersection where compassion and theology evolve into a smile. His congregational Christmas experiences unfold in stories that will stir your own memory of the holiday and encourage you to reflect on the nature of a relationship lived in faith. Angels abound; you are about to meet just a few of them. You will be blessed! I was!"

—RANDY JESSEN, EXECUTIVE DIRECTOR, GLOBAL HOPE

Angels We Have Heard Are High

Angels We Have Heard Are High

Stories That Bring Christmas Down to Earth

CHARLES SCHUSTER

RESOURCE *Publications* · Eugene, Oregon

ANGELS WE HAVE HEARD ARE HIGH
Stories That Bring Christmas Down to Earth

Resource Publications
An Imprint of Wipf and Stock Publishers
199 W. 8th Ave., Suite 3
Eugene, OR 97401

www.wipfandstock.com

PAPERBACK ISBN: 978-1-7252-8883-6
HARDCOVER ISBN: 978-1-7252-8884-3
EBOOK ISBN: 978-1-7252-8885-0

01/28/21

Contents

Introduction

As a pastor, I have seen many Advent/Christmas seasons come and go. I have been a witness to many children's Christmas pageants and plays, and have watched children in the act of trying to reenact the story of the birth of the Christ Child. They have disrupted and interrupted the program in a way that made the reenactment more real and more memorable than it would have been had the lines been spoken the way they were written.

I remember the little girl, named Jill, who walked into the Sanctuary as an angel, complete with wings and a halo. When she saw the light shining from the manger, she let out the most beautiful word of any spoken in the whole 30-minute play. Her word was "Wow!" The printed word cannot convey the impact of her show-stopping response. It was awe inspired.

I remember the year we used real babies for the Christ Child in the manger. They were twins and the babies were girls. We had a girl Jesus. We had two girl Jesuses. We had to take one of them out of the manger in the middle of the play and replace her with her sister. We did not want those kids to grow up with one saying to the other one, "I got to be Jesus, and you didn't."

One year we decided to have a live Nativity outside the Sanctuary on Christmas Eve. As the people came to church for the service, they walked past a makeshift shed and manger with Mary and Joseph, a few Shepherds, and three Wise Men. The local rancher supplied some farm animals. One of them was a goat whose name was Johnny. It was ever so cold, and it was snowing. The high school youth group that accepted the role of the Holy Family was ready for the exhibition to end so they could come in where it was warm and have hot chocolate and cookies as promised. They were not as ready to end the scene as the goat was. Johnny head-butted the angel and ran from the Manger scene through the door of the church and into the Sanctuary. The beginning of that service was delayed while we caught the goat and sent him back to the farm.

I recall one Christmas Pageant that had a moment that stopped the show. Right after one of the Magi said, "Let us go to Bethlehem and see this thing that has come to pass," one of the fifteen 4-year-old angels cried out in a voice that carried deep into the congregation, "I have to pee!" The scramble that ensued was especially impressive. His mother moved onto the stage with the speed of a linebacker, lifted him up, and made a dash to the restroom. She was too late, and we were one angel short for the remainder of the play.

I remember asking the children in a Children's Sermon the first Sunday in December if they knew what season of the Church year had begun. We had the Sanctuary decorated. We had Christmas trees and banners, and the purple vestments of the Season of Advent were in place.

"What season of the church are we in?" I asked.

One child, so proud of himself, said to me and everyone else that Sunday morning, "We are in the season of Advil." He was more correct than he knew. I'd had a headache that morning!

The stories of children and Christmas need to be told. For the hard-hearted skeptics there is a melting of the ice, a softening of the cynicism, and a weakening of the resistance to the idea of forces and factors greater than ourselves.

My intent with this book is to bring to life the Spirit of Christmas, as experienced by people in a variety of ways. I mean to do this because I think it is needed. Our nation has become polarized and paralyzed by our need to defend ourselves against those who disagree with us. We have gone through another one of those times when we live in a confusing present and an uncertain future. Words we have never heard are being used in a common vernacular. When, in our recent history, did we use the word "pandemic"?

Would we have ever imagined there could be "quarantining"? What would we have thought if the words "social distancing" had been used? How can we be social at a distance? Added to all this, we have seen school shootings, riots in the streets, recession, floods, global warming, and world conflict.

If there has ever been a time when we needed to hear, read, relive, and experience the Christmas story, it is now. Why is that the case? The Christmas story is one of those universal messages that transcends religious affiliations, political bias, and theological difference. The Christmas story is a reminder that if we believe "The Word became flesh and dwelt among us," we don't have to be less human to recognize the Godlike-ness within us. Our humanity is recognized and honored. Beyond the words and reciting of the narrative, Christmas is an experience of softness and love and beauty and hope. It brings light to our darkness, music to our ears, and love to our hearts.

If we accept the story of the birth of the Christ Child as a myth with a message, if we look for the Truth conveyed, and give up trying to prove that what is reported is literal fact, then we will find manifestations of the story in such things as a squirrel on the street corner, a pair of shoes that don't fit, and the secret of a shepherd girl.

I hope you enjoy reading my stories. More than that, I hope my book will call to mind your stories, and then, I hope you will write *your* book. Angels we have heard are high.

The Year Christmas Came to the Shady Rest Nursing Home

THERE COMES A TIME in life when the little things are not little, like when the slightest act of kindness has a profound effect, or when the most unintended rebuff has the lingering impact of a slap in the face. There comes a time when we realize we are not to ourselves, but we begin to tap into a power of something we know is present with us, even though we may not be able to describe it or name it. Theologians and preachers call this (power) "God."

Is there a lonelier place on Christmas Eve than to be alone, without a family, in a nursing home? This story is fiction, and yet, it is fact. It is a story about one woman, but it could be about any woman or man who feels alone and sad in the darkest time of year, when others are happy and filled with joy. . .

What is it about snow? What is it about snow on red brick and trees in the darkness of winter? They said there was a blizzard in the forecast. The police were encouraging people to stay home. Most people ignored the warning because they found a higher kind of encouragement with the prospect of snow flying in the air. The only disappointment was that the snow had not yet come.

However, some snow had fallen, and the roads were covered in white. It was a light, happy texture, like powdered sugar or cotton balls. The town took on the look of a Christmas scene from Currier and Ives. You could imagine horse-drawn sleighs and hot chocolate and happy greetings as people passed each other, talking about the measure of the white froth that had salted into small drifts. Smoke rose from the chimney stacks as people burned another layer of wood that they had cut in the fall of the year. Inside their homes, the crackle of the fire and the aspirations of those who stood or sat and watched, transfixed by the flicker of the blaze, seemed to remind people of a simpler time; it called them back to loved ones gone and buried and to those who were not buried, but who were all but gone.

The Shady Rest Nursing Home had been in its present spot for ten years. In prior years, it had been in the middle of town, concealed in a grove of cottonwood trees. Its present location on the top of a hill overlooked a long, lush valley. The background view was tall mountains, which in winter and in summer were capped with snow. As places like these go, Shady Rest was nice. It was clean and the employees were neat and caring. Generally, it was a cheerful place. It fit into the mystique of the scene and was an important part of the town's economy.

The Shady Rest Nursing home was made to look palatial and it was more than the look; it *was* palatial. The dining room was fashioned after a great hall in a mansion in England. There was wood on the walls and the tables were solid mahogany, enriched with a deep wood grain. Family crests, with symbols like sheep and snakes and lions and gazelles, lined the room. There were family slogans that would have made any person proud had they had that heritage. How can you not be proud of a family crest that reads, "Don't Tread on Me" or "We stand up for what is right when others cower in fear"? There was the Cameron Clan, the O'Donnell Clan, the Mosier Clan ensconced permanently on the walls. Since everybody has some kind of heritage, the residents were encouraged to find or design a family crest with which they could identify. The Shady Rest managers felt it was a good thing for the residents to be thinking beyond their own diminishing lives to something worthy of a crest, a symbol, or a slogan. Many of them participated vigorously. However, some thought this was contrived and resisted rather vociferously, in some cases, obnoxiously.

There was the night at the beginning of December when the residents were gathered and invited to answer the question, "If your family heritage had a crest, what would the symbol be and what would be the inscription?"

It was going well. One woman said her crest would read, "We never let the method outshine the moment, and the symbol would be a rose. It would tell the world, that we take the time to smell the roses." Another resident said his crest would read, "First to volunteer when the job needed done" and the symbol would be an ant.

All was good and the Activities Director and the Retirement Home manager were feeling that progress had been made; the residents were jovial and communicative. Well, *almost all* the residents were cheered by the games being played and there was a generally positive spirit with the residents.

December was moving toward the usual darkness of night and the bright expectation of the coming of Christmas. The town and staff had big plans for Christmas Eve. How is it possible to miss the spirit of Christmas? In the darkest time of year there is a need to remember the brightness of the light and to become reacquainted with the fact that no darkness, however deep, could defeat the light, however dim. This particular year, there was great need for the Christmas message. It had been a year of disease, and quarantine, and anger and riots, and general chaos. This was one of those years when everyone wanted and needed Christmas and almost everyone in the Shady Rest Nursing Home was coming under the spell of Christmas and the joy, hope, love, and beauty of the season.

However, there was this one resident who was generally difficult. She was morose and sullen on her best day. Most of the time she would snap at the other residents, call the nurses fat, and make unkind comments about the cooks and the food. She accused the kitchen staff of creating menus that were unfit for human consumption. One evening at the beginning of December she threw her plate of lasagna on the floor and shouted, "You are making us dig our graves with our teeth!"

The staff had tried everything to please her. They humored her, they ignored her hurtful comments and her acid tongue. They tried to get her counseling and even threatened to put her in the locked ward.

Her name was Ella Marie, although most people at the Retirement Center called her "Honey," or "Sweetheart," or "Sweetie," even though she was anything but sweet. She was a long-time resident of the Shady Rest Nursing Home, having lived there for over five years.

She had no close family. Perhaps, she had driven whatever family she had away. No one knew. No one came to see her. She had been placed there by a distant relative, who sought to do what was best, and this seemed to be best. Her needs and wants were provided. Her health was good, especially for one who has been 95 years on this Earth.

Christmas time at Shady Rest was an event that was important to the entire community. People came in from the outside to witness the live nativity, to sing Christmas carols, hear the Christmas story, and to give the residents their gifts. It was the only live nativity portrayal in the county, and the actors were chosen with care. The live participants took their places. There was Mary and Joseph, cattle, sheep, a donkey, magi, and shepherds. It was too cold for a baby, a real live infant, so a plastic doll played the part of the baby Jesus. A group from the high school came to sing, along with a quartet from the Baptist Church. The Baptist preacher gave a meditation. He came to officiate this big event.

The residents were being gathered for the Christmas Show. Some of them walked independently and some had canes. Some used walkers, and some were in wheelchairs. The residents were being brought onto the lawn in the cool December night. They were bundled up to withstand the cool of the midwinter. There was the prediction of snow.

There is something special about snow on Christmas Eve. Why is that? Most probably, Jesus was born in the Spring, if the story is to be held as true. Shepherds out in the field with sheep were there to protect the lambs from wolves. Does it really matter if the story is true or is it more important to know the story of Jesus' birth as conveying truth?

Snow on Christmas Eve seemed to bring a level of excitement to the Shady Rest Nursing Home. There was a buzz in the air.

Ella Marie was watching the national news when someone grabbed on to the back of her chair and propelled her toward the door. She offered no resistance, though she had no choice. Off she went. The orderly muttered not a word, the corridors and hallways began to blur, and she was a little dizzy because of the speed.

"*Look* at me," she thought to herself, as she stared back at the orderly, who was in such a hurry to get her down the hall and out the door. He remained silent and unresponsive to her unspoken wish. It was as if he was carting a bag of pinto beans through a warehouse. She was his obligation and his task.

"*Look* at me!" she thought, "*Who do you think I am*? I'm not just a cranky old woman who dribbles her food, who is uncertain of mood, or unclear of mind. Look at me. I was once a small child. I had a father and a mother, and I had brothers and sisters. I had a home that was happy. Look at me, Mister. I was once pretty, and I had places to go. When I'd walk into a room, people like you would turn and look. Look at me. I once was a bride. Life was good to me. I walked down the aisle of a church. Life was good to me until the dark days came, and my husband died in the War. I have his picture, that is all, and it is a faint memory of what I was to him, and what he was to me. I cling to that picture and I try to remember.

"*Look* at me. I'm more than an old woman with cracks in her face and with a sour disposition. I won't eat green beans, but I never liked green beans. My heart seems like stone. When you get old, you go through hard times. You accept what you must accept, but it's not easy.

"*Look* at me, as you shove your cart with me in it. Please, look at me. I am somebody. I was somebody; I still am somebody. *Look at me.*"

Ella Marie was brought to a spot in front of a fountain. Her chair, with the others, formed a half circle. One of the nurses walked over to Ella Marie's chair, looked deeply into her eyes, and said with great ceremony, "For you."

She gave her a box. It was a pretty box. It was covered with red and green paper and it was tied up with a bright gold bow. Inside, there was an ornament with silver tinsel and shimmering fringe.

The pastor from the Baptist Church was beginning his Meditation. He read the text in Greek and then he read the text in English. The text said, "And the Word became flesh." And he said, "No matter how you read it, it says the same thing. It says, *This* is for you. It suggests that the Word of God is given for you. It tells us what has come to us. It says, "This is for you."

"For me?" she thought, "Oh God, for me. They are doing this for me! How many years I've done for others! How many people I've helped! How many times I've taken the time to help! Helping was what I did. I wasn't a lawyer, or a doctor, or a pastor, or a priest. I read the Bible and understood that we are called to be helpers. We are commanded to be caring."

"This is for me. For me," she thought. The tears began to flow, and the tears and the tinsel flowed together. The thing that hurt her most was that she was no longer a helper.

"This is for me. Oh God, *for me?* The word became flesh. I wish there were not so many things done for me. The word became flesh for me. The child was born for me. The Scriptures were read for me. The carols were sung for me. Dinner is served for me. Pills are given for me. People are kind for me. They do it all for me. What can I do when I can't help? Why is everything done for me?"

The pastor pointed to the child in the manger. Again, he read in the Greek. He translated into English in a variety of ways, "The word became flesh and cohabitated with us. The word became flesh and lived with us. The word became flesh and took up residency with us. The word became flesh and dwelt among us."

"Look at the child," the pastor continued, "It's a plastic replica. His hair is long, and it is in locks. His arms are spread, and his mouth is open in prayer. His eyes are bright. Look at this child and you also see something surprising. There is a belt around his waist. It is a leather belt. Every year somebody tries to take the baby. This year the baby is tied down. He dwells among us. He is tied into the Earth with us."

Ella Marie thought of all the times they had tied her down. They called it a restraint, and they said it was for her good. She had been tied down and, as she looked at the baby in the manger, she felt something she had never felt before. It was something about herself and about her God. It was something about her stubborn nature and something about Jesus' stubborn nature. This child was tied down by a shackle so firm that he couldn't escape. And yet that child had lived a life so free that nobody could tie him down.

They wanted a political savior, and he sought to save their souls. They wanted a mouthpiece to promote the pious life of peace, and he gave them words that agitated the masses.

Ella Marie thought about the way her life had been tied down through the ravages of age. Her own stubborn nature kept her alive. *His* stubborn nature kept him true to the word that became flesh, through him, and that dwelt among us. Seeing that baby tied down made her feel something she had not felt in years. She felt free.

She looked around the circle and saw all the people. She looked them in the eye. The children who were there were so expectant. She watched people from the school, and their faces seemed so full of love. The pastor, and the nurses, the orderlies, and the people who ran the Home, and the other residents—they had no malice in their hearts. They had no hatred.

She saw for the first time that the Christ Child was tied down like *she* was tied down. He dwelt where she dwells. She recalled that they even had to tie him down on the cross to keep him in his place. He dwells among us. He was tied down with us.

Just before she was wheeled back to her room, Ella Marie looked once more at the leather strap that held the child in his place. She thought of his life and how many people would rather have worshipped a Christ in a crib, taking him sentimentally as a baby when he was born, but not seriously later, as the prophet he became. She thought about his life and how they tried to tie him down. They found they couldn't do it and then, and only then, did they worship him as Christ.

"He came off the cross and out of the crib to be with me," she thought.

"His stubborn nature inspires mine," she thought.

"His broken body heals my broken spirit," she thought.

She thought of her life and about the importance of the struggle and how the struggle was so significant because of the meaning it gives. The human spirit has its divine quality, which comes from not giving in, or giving up. It comes in not quitting when things are tough. She thought of her own stubborn nature, and she resolved to make the best of the days she had left.

"If I cannot help with my hands, maybe I can help with a smile or an attitude or a kind word. He is with me," she thought. "This child is with me. This child, in a manger, *is with me.* This infant, who had been strapped to the wood, *is with me.* . .and, because He is with me, I am not alone. The world is not so frightening. The future is not so grim. My aches and pains don't hurt any less, but they mean something now, because He is with me," she thought.

As they wheeled her back to her room the discontented posture seemed to subside. The combativeness was beginning to give way to something of a softer look. She gazed out the window and she saw that the snow was piling up and it covered the manger scene. It covered the little shed they had built to replicate the barn. They had said he was born in a stable. It covered the Magi, the astrologers from the East who said they were Wise Men. It covered their turbans. It covered the shepherds and the sheep and the cows and the other animals. They said Jesus was put in a feed trough. She looked and she saw it. The snow had covered the manger. It covered where the child was placed. The child was there but the snow covered the leather strap that was put there to hold the child down.

Suddenly words she had heard for years began to make sense for the very first time in her life: "The Word was made flesh and dwells among us." The Word was made flesh and it dwells in her. The spirit of Christmas was in her. Christmas and the birth of the Christ Child had become a reality—a Truth. No longer was it an abstraction.

Ella Marie knew the truth of the child in the manger. As for the leather strap and the theft of the child, she knew it really didn't matter. No one could steal that child this year. He was in Ella Marie's heart.

She now understood, in a new way, the Word, and that it had come to dwell among us. Christmas had come to the Shady Rest Nursing Home.

Ella Marie did something she had not done in months, maybe years. She smiled. There was "peace on earth." At least there was peace in the heart of one of the residents of the Shady Rest Nursing Home.

The Shepherd Girl's Story

WAS THE CHRIST CHILD the only child in the story of the birth of Jesus? Were there other children? Is it possible to imagine another child who came to the manger to see the miracle of this birth?

I think that is possible. If there is any truth to the story, there had to be another child. Maybe it was a child from the Inn or from the little town of Bethlehem. Perhaps there were children helping the Innkeeper feed the animals in the stable.

I think there was a child who came to the Inn, who saw the baby, and at the time had no idea what she had seen. But I think there was something she heard. It was the sound that is heard by the heart. It is the sound that silence makes. I think there was a shepherd's daughter in Bethlehem that night when the Christ Child was born. I think she had a story to tell, and if she told the story, this is what it would have been. . .

I share a story with you. It is the sound that silence makes. It is the story of a shepherd girl, and it is a story about her gift.

Now you have never heard the story of the shepherd girl because, up to now, it has never been told. You have never met the shepherd girl because, up to now, she has never been known.

A long time ago there was a woman who lived in the town of Bethlehem. She had grown quite old. She had lived a full and rich life, but a life with its share of sadness. She was a widow; her husband had died some years before. She had children, grandchildren and she had a secret. It was a secret she had never shared until one day near the end of her days, she called her family together to tell them what was in her heart.

They gathered around her bed. The old woman, who had lived a long, long time, told her story of the sound that silence makes. This was her story.

"Children, friends, family, my dear, dear children," she said. "My dear, dear friends, you are my life. You are all that matters to me now and before I die there is something I must tell you. . .

It happened long, long ago. I haven't told a soul. My father, your grandfather, was a shepherd and that, I know you know. He, on occasion, would let me go out with him into the field. It was a special treat for me to be with him and the others to watch our flock and to listen to the stillness of the night, and to watch the brilliant beauty of the stars: the little dots of light that shined defiant against the dark.

Our job was to protect the sheep from wolves and robbers by night and day. I so looked forward to being there with him. I found it so peaceful to sit out under the stars and to hear the sound that silence makes.

Let me tell you about this one night that happened 73 years ago. There was a light in the sky. It was a bright blue light. It was almost blinding and yet, in a way, it was a clearing of the eyes to new vision. There were voices singing. The silence itself was speaking. . .spoken to us shepherds, spoken to my father and to me, sung by the silence of the night through the wind and the breezes whistling through the grass and trees, sung by the voices in the sky.

We were urged to go to Bethlehem. We were invited by the sound that silence made to follow the star. All of us wanted to go because all of us felt compelled to give in to our intuitions. But, you see, some of us had to stay behind with the flock. Some of us had to keep watch over the flock. Some of us could not go see this thing which had come to pass. Some of us *would* not go because we were afraid.

My father volunteered to stay with the flock, not because he was afraid, but because that's the kind of man he was. He was always thinking of others first. I remember how disappointed I was for myself and even more for my father. I was 12 years old at the time and the idea of seeing God in the form of a child excited me beyond imagination. Somehow this child was born for me.

But my father was the one I hurt for the most. He had, all his life, been looking for something, and he had been hoping to be a part of something important. Shepherds were looked down upon by people in those days and my father was ridiculed by his family. It was assumed he would have, or should have, carved out a better life for my mother and me. He was restless and he loved the outdoor life. But there was something in his life that was missing. Outside in the wilderness, however, he seemed most content. He searched the heavens and he listened to the sound that silence makes. It's too bad he couldn't go to Bethlehem. He chose to stay behind.

I could not sleep that night. It was a clear, crisp, cool night. The animals were restless, as if they knew something big was about to happen. Later, I heard the shepherds return, and I listened as they told what they had seen. I awakened my father and asked if we could go see for ourselves, but he would not hear of it. After all, what was described could hardly be believed to be the birth of a King: a peasant child, wrapped in swaddling clothes, lying in a manger because there was no room in the Inn. No King would have been born like that. I asked if I could go alone to see the babe and my father would not even consider it. He said the dangers were many and I was a child of 12.

What happened next, I have not told a single soul; now, I'm telling you. I disobeyed my father. I waited till he went back to sleep, and I left. I slipped out in the dark and, for some strange reason, I took with me a lamb. I made the journey into town and followed the trail toward the Inn. I circled back behind the Inn to the cave where I saw the Holy Family. There was a large man, standing near the manger and speaking in a soft voice. His arms were big and strong, and his head and beard were trimmed, but his clothes were threadbare, betraying the fact that he was of peasant stock.

The mother of the child was holding the baby in her arms, and there was such a look upon her face. It was a panicked look; it was the pain of being human, I have later thought. But there was also a look of a different sort; there was joy in her eyes. I have later thought it was the joy of knowing much more than humans ever know.

I saw the child. It was a boy. It was their son. I looked at him to see if I could tell, by looking, that he was special, divine, or different. I looked for lights and halos. I listened for voices, like those we had heard in the field, but I saw nothing. I heard nothing; it was just the sound silence makes. In fact, the most striking feature about this scene was that there was nothing striking about it. He was so ordinary. He was so plain, so humble. It could not have been that this child was the Messiah. It could not have been. It was not possible.

The lamb in my arms began to struggle, and it raced through my mind to keep the gift. This was surely some mistake because this was no Messiah. Just as I turned to walk away and prepared to leave, I looked into the eyes of the child, and I saw something no mere human eye can quite possess. I saw love; there was such love in the eye of the child. I saw love, and I heard the sound the silence makes.

"This is my gift and it's for you," I said. "This is my gift."

The mother spoke to me and she was not much older than I. She said, "My son will not forget you."

I left shortly after that, and I wondered, "Have I seen the King of Kings? Had I not? Was this a hoax?" Had it not been for the look of that child and had it not been for the sound I heard, the sound that silence makes, I would have dismissed the happening as a cruel prank.

That was years ago, and I told no one, and no one noticed that the lamb was gone. What is one lamb among so many? Yet the look of that child haunted me for years. It was disturbing. Later I was married, had children, and moved to Jerusalem. I had the usual ups and downs. My husband died years ago. His death was tragic and unexpected. I was left a widow. I was left to mourn his death, and to try to keep my life together. There were days, and perhaps years, I barely made it through. I was lost and alone, disturbed, stricken, and sad. My friends tried to help, but I knew this was my journey to walk, my life to live, my burden to carry. I'd wake in the night, disoriented, confused, and yet, seeing the child's face, hearing the sound that silence makes, gave me consolation in those dark and desperate years of grief.

One day, on the way into town, I saw a crowd of people. Some of them were standing, and some of them were sitting down. They were listening to this man as he spoke, and several of them were questioning some of what he said.

They said to him, "Why do you eat with outcasts? Why do you associate with sinners? Why do you mix with the poor? Who do you think you are? What is God? Who are you to God? Who are you?"

I walked up to the crowd, and He looked at me. There was something about his eyes, as if I had seen him before. I *had* seen him somewhere, sometime. He looked at me as if he knew who I was and, when he spoke, I heard the sound that silence makes again. Chills ran up and down my back.

"Love. . .," he said to us, "love is the secret to life. Love the Lord your God. Love your neighbor as yourself. I have come to bring life. I have come to bring abundant life. I am here to teach love as a way to live. If you wish to save your life, give it away to causes bigger than yourselves.

You ask me who I am," he said, "I am the good shepherd. Think of me this way and, like a good shepherd, my flock knows my voice. I have come to find lost sheep and to show them the way of love. I am here to help the lost be found, and to show them new life. I am like a good shepherd."

Was he the child I had seen there in the manger? Was he the child in Bethlehem that day? If so. . .if so, could it be that my gift, the gift of an insignificant shepherd girl, was what he needed, to learn who he was? Was it my gift that helped him understand the kind of King he would become?

He was "King" of all Kings, but his approach to being King was different. He was like a shepherd. It was the magnetism of his smile, and his humble manner; it was the kindness in his eyes and his faith in God. What I saw in the manger when he was born, and what I saw on the hillside when he spoke, and what made him great, was his meekness. What made him King was his servant quality. What made him "God-like" was his loving care for his flock. His sense of kindness was contagious.

Was it my gift to him that helped make him so?

This thought I leave for you at this time of year when it is darkest. It is an idea that helped me so much when I was lost and hurting: When things do not go the way they should, and you wake up at night restless and upset, feeling like you don't count for much, listen for the sound that silence makes.

This is what I have come to understand. When I am feeling alone and sad, there is something that points me to look to the stars, and all the little dots of light in the sky. Each light in the darkness is a symbol of a person you have helped along the way; and the more people you have helped, the bigger your sky, and the brighter your stars.

That sound silence makes is a word and the word is love. That sound the silence makes points us to the stars, and encourages us to light our candles, and to stand against the darkness. No darkness can defeat the light. It seems to me, what I saw in that stable in the back of that Inn in Bethlehem, was light, because I do not remember how dark it was. What I remember is how fortunate I have been, and what a privilege I have had to live my life trying to have influence for good. I will never forget the look of love and kindness in the eyes of that child, or in the eyes of the man he became. I knew he was special. I wanted you all to know my story."

The old woman stopped speaking and it got noticeably quiet. Her family was stunned by what they had heard. There wasn't much that needed to be said, and no one spoke as they embraced her.

One of her grandchildren, Abraham, walked over to his grandmother and said to her, "The look of love on the face of the child, and the look of kindness you thought you saw on the one they call Jesus, is something I, too, have seen. I have seen it in your eyes. There is something special about you, Grandmother. There has always been something special about you. Now I know what it is."

In the silence that followed all agreed that they had seen it too. It seems to be true. When we look at "pure love and kindness," it is contagious.

A Story for Children at Christmas

CHRISTMAS IS FOR CHILDREN, but it is for children of all ages. Every person has a bit of childlikeness. Jesus spoke of the Realm of God as having been offered for children. I think he implied that the Kingdom of God is for children of every age. Some young people seem old and some old people seem young; but there is a child in every person, no matter their age. This is best understood as it relates to giving and receiving. Christmas is a time to give and receive gifts. It involves us in one of the most interesting paradoxes we experience. The more we give, the more we get. The more we have, the greater the privilege of giving it away. It is also true that people who are accustomed to giving must learn to be recipients of other people's gifts.

All this is a jumble of theological circular thinking that is best expressed in a story. This is a story that never happened, and yet, it happens often. It is a story about a poor child who is rich. It is a story about the wisdom of youth and the kindness of the adult world. It is a story about the little bit that is much, and how Christmas reminds us that our purpose on earth is to know who we are, so we can give of ourselves, and to see what we have, so we can respond to human need. It is a story about giving and receiving and the power of a good example...

School! Some of the most interesting things happen at school. There was the day Benjamin Snodgrass put the snake in Mrs. Hortence Fisher's desk drawer, and when she saw it, she kicked the trash can over three rows of 5th grade students. After the can hit the back wall, five of the students stood with their hands in the air like referees at a football game, indicating the field goal was good!

Then there was the day last April when somebody super-glued all the doors shut, and the fire department had to come to get the building open so classes could begin after Spring vacation.

Let me tell you the most interesting thing that happened at Burbaker Grade School this past year. It involved a little girl, a little girl named Jessie. The small town had fallen on hard times. Lots of people did not have jobs and when you don't have a job, you don't have a paycheck. When that happens this time of year, it means some of the children won't be able to have much of a Christmas.

The Principal of the school, Mr. Dillard, was always having ideas. Many of them were strange ideas. Mr. Dillard was like a child in many respects. Some of his ideas were absurd. Once he thought it would be a great thing if all the male teachers grew beards and all the female teachers shaved the hair off the top of their heads. Four teachers threatened to quit. Once he thought it would be a fun thing on Thanksgiving to get up in a helicopter and drop live turkeys down onto the parent teacher conferences. But it turned out to be a terrible thing, when it was discovered that turkeys can't fly if they weigh over thirty pounds.

One of his best ideas was to collect money for the families of the children in the school who would be having a meager Christmas. In early December, Mr. Dillard called all the children together in the auditorium and told them the plan.

"We're going to collect money for the children who are less fortunate, so they will have something to open on Christmas Day," Mr. Dillard said. "We're going to have your parents send you to school with some money; we want you to bring it to school the last day before Christmas vacation." As he looked at the children his eyes fell on little Jessie. Mr. Dillard thought about Jessie. He knew about her parents. He knew how sick her mother had been and how she hadn't been able to work. He knew how Jessie's father couldn't get work as a carpenter because nobody had enough money to build a house. Mr. Dillard thought of Jessie as he went on to explain, "Now, we're going to make a Nativity Scene here in front of the school. We're going to have a manger with a baby in it."

Several of the other teachers thought of Jessie, as Mr. Dillard talked about how sad it was going to be for some of the children this Christmas. Mrs. Alford was Jessie's homeroom teacher. She too thought how sad it would be for Jessie this Christmas, and she made a promise to herself to put in extra money so children, like Jessie, would have some gifts to open at Christmas.

Mr. Dillard continued talking as the children became noticeably quiet. "We're going to have Mary, the mother of Jesus, and we're going to put her beside the manger. We'll have to find a blanket to wrap the baby up in swaddling clothes."

Jessie said it out loud and everybody heard her say it: "I could bring the blanket my mother made. I could put it in the manger."

Nobody said a word to Jessie. They just kind of ignored her.

Mr. Dillard continued, "We're going to have Joseph here by the manger. Joseph was the baby's father and Joseph was a carpenter."

Jessie said out loud, and everybody heard her say it, "My father is a carpenter. I could bring some of his work clothes, and I could ask him to build a shelter for the baby. He would be happy to have something to do." Nobody said a word to Jessie. They just kind of ignored her.

Mr. Dillard and Mrs. Alford, and all the other children and teachers thought about Jessie. They knew that Jessie would be one of the kids whose families would be getting gifts from the manger, after they had collected the money. Jessie and her family were poor, you see.

Mr. Dillard went on to say, "We'll have shepherds at the manger, and we will have kings from the East at the manger. The Magi or Kings brought gifts to baby Jesus and, in the same way, we will bring gifts for the poor.

Jessie said it, and everybody heard her say it, "I want to give money for poor children. I have money for my lunch. I want to give money for the poor. I have money I bring for my lunch every day. I could save it and give it to the poor."

Everyone heard her say it, but everyone ignored her, because she was poor. They knew the money they were collecting was for children like her and her family.

A Story for Children at Christmas

It came to pass. There was the Baby, Mary and Joseph, and some sheep, and a manger. Mr. Dillard and the other teachers looked at the manger scene and thought it looked wonderful, but there seemed to be something missing. They didn't know what it was, but something was not quite right. It was a week before Christmas, and the children were to bring their money the last day of school, just before Christmas vacation.

On the day before the last day of class, before Christmas vacation, something very strange happened. First it started to rain. It was a cold rain; you know, the kind of rain that falls straight down and hits the ground hard and bounces. It was the kind of rain that makes you want to stay inside, and makes you want to drink hot chocolate, and put some marshmallows in it. It makes you want to sit by a fire and read a good book, and get under a blanket, and think about things. It was that kind of rain. Then it started to do something else. It began to turn white. The rain began to turn to snow. The snow fell, and it snowed, and it snowed some more.

Then, guess what? It snowed so much that the streets were filled with snow. It snowed so much that Mr. Dillard and Mrs. Alford and the teachers and some of the parents got together and, you know what? They decided to call off school on the day before Christmas vacation. They called the radio stations, and they called the television stations, and they put the word out on the school's webpage. The message said, "No school today. See you next year."

The children were not sad. Some of them thought it would be great fun to go sled riding down the big hill north of town. Some of them thought it would be wonderful just to stay inside, and drink hot chocolate with marshmallows, sit by a fire, and read a good book. Some of the children thought it would be fun to build a snowman and a snow woman. Nobody had ever built a snow couple.

Believe it or not, nobody was disappointed that Mr. Dillard had called off school—except Mr. Dillard. He went around his house pacing back and forth, and muttering under his breath. He wondered about the children, and what they would miss if they could not come to school. He worried about the school building. He worried about whether all the doors were locked, and if there was heat in the building so the pipes would not freeze. He worried about lots of things, and he was driving Mrs. Dillard crazy. Finally, she said to him, "Well, Daniel, why don't you walk over to the school? You're not doing me any good standing there looking out the window or pacing the floor."

Mr. Dillard lived four blocks from the school, and he decided to walk over to the school, despite the weather conditions that had now become a blizzard of snow and wind. The snow was so deep that he could barely walk, and he could not have driven. It took him almost an hour to get there. The snow was so deep, he didn't think he had ever seen a snow like this one. When he got to the school, he checked all the doors. He checked out the furnace. He was just about to leave when he thought about the manger and Mary and Joseph, and the shepherds and the wise men, and the baby Jesus. He thought about the gifts for the children; he was sad that the snow had come, and that there wouldn't be any gifts for the poor children that year.

When he got to the manger in front of the school, he was surprised to see how much snow had piled up on the figures of Mary and Joseph, the shepherds, the wise men, and even the baby Jesus. He looked at the scene and it was then that he realized what was missing. Angels! He had forgotten to put angels into the scene. He took out his little book, and he wrote "angels" in the book so next year he would remember.

He looked out across the playground, covered with snow, and he investigated the street, and he thought he saw tracks in the snow. The snow had almost covered the tracks, but not quite. He looked down at the manger and, as he did, he saw a cloth sack of coins. It must be a bag of money for the poor children!

Despite the snow, on a day in which school was cancelled, someone had put a bag of money into the manger. Who was it? Who put the money in the manger on the day before Christmas vacation? He thought he knew who it was who could have put the money in the manger for poor children, but he wanted to be sure. He went back to his office and he called Mrs. Alford, and he told her what had happened.

"Mrs. Alford, who do you think put the bag of money in the manger? You don't suppose it was J. . .?" He didn't finish.

Mrs. Alford said to him, "And we all thought we didn't have an angel in the Manger Scene this year. Well, we were wrong. We did have an angel."

She continued, "I came over to the school earlier today and I noticed the blanket that covered the baby Jesus. It was put there by an angel. Remember the child who talked about her mother who made a blanket, and how she would bring it to the school so the baby would be wrapped in swaddling clothes? Do you remember the name of that child? Her name was Jessie. She was the angel, and as I saw her walking away from the school, I thought I heard a voice say, "Glory to God in the highest and on earth, peace, and good will."

Whenever we go to sleep on the night of the first day of Christmas vacation, right before Christmas day, we might want to remember the story of the school and the Christmas Manger scene. We may receive presents, and we may have presents to give. Remember the little girl named Jessie, whose mother was sick, and her father was a carpenter. The thing about Christmas we will always remember is this: you never know who is rich and who is poor. As we remember the story of Christmas, angels always appear. They are the ones who give more than they have, and who care to make things better for everyone.

Christ and Crystal

Every so often something happens that causes questions to be asked that are deep and disturbing. Assumptions, fervently held, no longer hold. Core beliefs, once embraced with certainty, become vulnerable to the skeptic's challenge. Is there anything about the Christmas message that speaks to death or dying? Is there a relationship between Bethlehem, the little town, and bedlam, the chaotic and tragic quality life takes at times?

A young couple with a sick little girl came to the church I was serving in 1980. The child was four. She had already undergone several surgeries and was to face many more. Her name was Crystal. Her story and the birth of the Christ Child and the danger his life would face seemed to merit further thought. The illness and struggle of a little girl, and the situation that she and her parents faced, could be tragic and it was tragic in many ways. But there was something special about this child. She was such a positive spirit. In her dying, she gave life. In contrast, the Christ Child's birth was established to be God's statement about how life leads to death, but how death leads to resurrection. The mystery of life and death is the underlying theme of this story:

While it is painful to think of the illness of a child at Christmas, this story represents the power of love, and enables us to face the darkness with the light of hope that Christmas always brings.

Christmas comes at the darkest time of year. Christmas represents the idea of God coming in the form of a child, to be present with

us in that darkness. The answer to the question, O God, do you care?
is, "Immanuel, God is with us."

There is one card I received at Christmas that came in the usual way and I opened it in the usual way and read the message. The message on the card was a usual kind of message. It read, "Remember the word Immanuel." There was a picture of one angel and a child. What was unusual about that card was that it had no name. It was unsigned. I don't know the name of the sender; just the message, "Remember the word Immanuel." Remember that "God is with us." That's what the word Immanuel means—"God is with us."

There is one person to whom I would like to send that card, but I don't know her name, nor do I know where I'd send it.

It was late on Christmas Eve, or by then, it was Christmas Day. It was 1:30 a.m. I am a preacher. Church was over. There had been three services, and the last one ended at 12 midnight. That's when it was supposed to end. The anthem was a little long. It took the ushers a while to distribute the candles. We started a bit late because the people were late getting there. The prelude droned on and on, and I could have cut the sermon some, but I didn't. I had completed the third worship service, and I was tired, and the snow was falling, and it was 1:30 in the morning, and the roads were becoming dangerous. and I was ready to be home.

I was loaded down with a bowl of water and two goldfish. It was a Christmas gift for my daughter who had wanted fish. She had wanted fish the previous year and I bought her a fossilized rock of a fish from the Paleolithic Age. This particular year she specified she wanted fish that were contemporary and alive.

So, the fish were swimming in the water, and the water was baptizing my arm. I was the last one to leave the building; exercising the prerogative, like a Captain being the last to leave a sinking ship, although the Christmas Eve services could better be described as rising hope. As a last gesture of compulsive obedience to my job, I opted to check the phone messages. I could not imagine there would be messages on the answering machine. Who calls a church after midnight? "Surely not," I thought. "Hopefully not," I prayed. I was wrong. My prayer was not answered. The light was indicative of the fact that a call had come in at one o'clock in the morning after the services had ended, and the people had left. So, after more church than anyone should have to experience, I decided to listen to one more voice. The voice was slurred and staggered and stunted by I wasn't sure what. Was it strong drink that made her sound the way she did? Was it her age? Was it overwhelming despair of a mood she could not understand much less control—a mood that had control of her? Who could know? I did not.

"Hello? Hello? Hello there? Oh, it's a recording," she said. "Is anybody there? Does anybody care about me?"

There was a voice in the background. It was a voice that was harsh and loutish. It was a voice that was impatient and cross. "Come on, Momma, it's just a church. There's *nobody* there."

The voice of the woman returned, and by now there were tears, "O God, don't you care? Don't you care about an old woman? Doesn't anybody care about an old woman? O God, don't you care? Doesn't anybody care?"

At this point the receiver went dead. The recorded message was over. Somehow, the fact that it was 1:30 in the morning, the dark became more a force than a fact, and the crisp winter evening that prompted warmth by the fireside where chestnuts would be roasting, now conjured up a chill that went to the bone. The empty recorder would not yield its purpose, which was stated in the recorded announcement, "You have reached First United Methodist Church. Your call is important to us but there is no one in the office just now. Please leave your name and number and do so at the sound of the tone. Have a Merry Christmas." Ping!

There was no number to call. There was no way to answer, "O God, don't you care? Doesn't anybody care? O God, don't you care?"

For 12 months that message has been a haunting benediction to a Christmas Eve worship. As a New Year's resolution, the church must resolve to hear the question should it come to us again. "O God, don't you care? Doesn't anybody care?" In so far as we could answer with our lives or, as a Church through its programs, we tried. With our words and our helping, and with our compassion and our silent listening, we tried to be the answer to that woman who called after hours on Christmas Eve and who raised that question, "O God, don't you care? Doesn't anybody care?"

Years later there *was* an answer to the question. There was a word that confronted the silence of that unanswered call. It spoke not to us, but through us. It spoke not for God, but from God. It was a word that answered the question, "O God, don't you care?"

What I am about to describe may be difficult, but it will be direct. What I'm about to suggest may be painful at first, but at the end of the day, it could be powerful. It may produce tears, but through the tears is the most amazing story of hope. . .

I met a little 4-year-old girl and her name was Crystal. Her father introduced us and I later met her mother. Crystal was a beautiful little girl and her beauty was much more than surface level, although on the surface alone, there was beauty. Her hair had been cut short. Crystal had done lots of things little girls had done. She had been lots of places other little girls had been, but there was something about her that was captivating; something that gets into your soul once you meet her. It won't let you go.

Her parents have pictures of her when she had long hair. There were pictures they took when she went to Disneyland and met Mickey and Goofy. Just looking at the pictures, it was hard to tell who the celebrity is.

What is tough to know about Crystal is that Crystal has a brain tumor. No, it's not malignant, but that doesn't matter. It's in a place in her brain where there is nothing the doctors can do. There have been major operations, but the doctors are out of options or ideas. Nobody knows for sure how long she will live. She has been near death three times, and each time that they revived her, the question comes: Why have we done it?

But let me tell you the rest of the story about this child whose spirit and beauty transcends her illness. It's about a little girl whose courage has touched her doctors in ways we could never describe. Crystal knows more about life and death than most of us will ever know or could ever claim to understand. She has been to death and back, and she describes beatific visions; her parents know she is not afraid. God is with her. She is not afraid.

This four-year-old is able to transcend her illness, and her greatest trauma is her worry over her parents, and their worry over her. Her favorite color is purple. When her father came to church that December, he noticed the purple colors in the church, and he thought of her. That's as it should be. Purple is the color of royalty and Crystal is a queen. There is a wisdom about this child that is a wisdom beyond her years. It is a wisdom beyond all years. A visit to her bedside is a visit to a hero who has looked death straight in the eye and hasn't blinked. The smile on her face is a determined saintliness, and a strength that proclaims the facts that only faith can know. It is a faith that says, good will triumph over evil; if you wait long enough, you will see it. Good will conquer bad; if you keep the faith, you will understand. Life will defeat death; if you look for the signs, you can see it.

God was present in that room where a child would soon die. God was there.

I asked her father for permission to tell Crystal's story, suggesting I would use a different name to conceal her identity. But he told me there was no need to do that. He said, "Please tell Crystal's story. Use her name if it will help someone else. Please do tell her story."

I asked her mother, "Do you see God in this?"

She answered, "I've had to rethink my ideas about God and the world. Crystal has taught me that there are realities so much bigger than the realities I know or can ever know. I've had to trust in a God who is bigger than my pain, to help me get through this. God is crying with us when we cry. Crystal has taught me to trust."

Crystal is our answer to the woman who called a year ago. Her life is at the very heart of Christmas. God is answering tragedy and trauma, not with formulae that will remove all doubt and answer all questions. God is responding to the hurt and heartache, using our doubts to mobilize our faith. As we sense God's presence, God activates healing where there is pain. And as we confront our most serious doubts, God revitalizes our search on a deeper level.

The God Christians believe in made his presence felt through the birth of a baby. In the manger God is alpha. God is beginning. God makes his presence felt as the illness of a child turns the patient into the therapist; as one for whom care is given becomes caretaker of those she loves. God is omega. God is at the ending.

The question posed on that Christmas Eve in the darkness of Christmas Day, "O God. . ..God do you care? Is anybody there? Does anybody care?"

The silence following the question has an answer that comes in time, and the silence is broken by the birth of a baby, and through the death of a child. The answer comes to us and through us, and it is from the God we worship, who is saying to us, in that silence, "I am with you. I am with you in your birth. I am with you in your death. I am with you when they stand and applaud your name. I am with you when they divert their eyes and step aside to avoid your acquaintance. I am with you in your loving days. I am with you in your lonely days. I am with you as you merge into a crowd, and I am with you when you stand alone. I am with you under the star-lit night. I am with you under the oxygen tent. I am with you as you stand proud of the achievement of your children. I am with you as you watch your children suffer and there is nothing to be done. The most painful time of all is to watch your child suffer."

And God said, "I watched my son suffer on a cross. I watch all my sons and daughters when they suffer, and the pain I know is the pain you know. I am with you. I am with you when the tears well up in your eyes to the point you can no longer see. I am with you when your love is far, far away. I am the bridge between lovers, so that time and distance, death and grief are defeated by a power that is at the core of creation: the power of love."

"God! O God!

Do you care?"

And God answers every Christmas. . .

"I am with you in life

I am with you in death

Birth—death

Alpha—Omega

Christ—Crystal"

There is a Christmas card sent every year and it looks un-signed, but it only looks unsigned. It reads, "Remember the word Immanuel! God is with us." It is signed "God," and it is addressed, "To whom it may concern."

Angels We Have Heard are High

THERE ARE TWO GROUPS *in any church that a wise preacher will never want to cross: the women's organization and the adult choir. Choir members do put in significant time practicing, and the sacrifice they make is notable. However, their exaggerated sense of worth can lead to tension, and this most often happens when an adult choir presents a 25-minute anthem, making a worship service go beyond the one-hour allotted time. No one will blame the choir for a long anthem when there is a preacher who proceeds to offer a regularly timed sermon as planned; or worse, when a preacher cuts the sermon to the point that its effectiveness is reduced.*

This story addresses, in a subliminal way, the various pathologies in the adult choir in one church. It also lifts the importance of the gift of music, and the importance of the singer and the song. Music is an expression of faith that is best presented through the sincerity of the singer rather than the precision of the notes. When the song is sung from the heart, the music conveys the message.

Sometimes, singers forget to sing from the heart. Sometimes choirs fail to tap into the power of the song. At Christmas time, however, most singers awaken to the beauty of the human voice, the power of the melody, and the meaning of the words.

This story expresses the convergence of such a time, and the reunion of heaven and earth in a moment of joy and hope.

The beauty of the season is accentuated by the poetic splendor of a choir at full voice, in a sanctuary adorned in pine, and with a

congregation eager to receive, once more, the arrival in reenactment of the birth of the Christ Child. We sing carols once a year.
We sing old ones we have sung for years. We sing new ones, recently
learned. The singing is both announcement of the mood and the
creation of the feeling appropriate to Christmas.

Did you ever wonder why? Why is it we sing carols at Christmas? We didn't always, you know. In the original story it was
only the angels who sang. As I understand it, this is the story as
it unfolded: Every year the chorus of angels gathered high up in
the heavens on the Sunday before Christmas. They gathered to sing
the annual serenade to the Christ Child. The songfest continued
throughout the remaining several days until the official celebration
of the blessed event itself. One might assume the angels' chorus was
the highest manifestation of perfection, and each year would be like
the next. Perfection has no room for the variable human factor. But,
of course, that assumption is wrong. Angels are people who have
discovered the divinity in being human—that's all.

So it was that some years the choir was better than other years.
Some years the bass section dominated, and the strength of the
voices inspired mere mortals to stand a little taller. When the bass
section was strong, repercussions sent ripples around the globe.
Those years were noted as years of faith. People were able to believe
again when the bass section was strong.

In other years it was the tenor section that monopolized, and
when that happened there was a different mood. The earth dwell-
ers heard the clarity of pitch, and they were inspired to order. It
takes discipline to be a tenor, and discipline leads to organization.
When the tenor section took the lead in the heavenly choir, people
began to sort out their lives. It would be a year of discipline and
organization.

Sometimes it was the alto section that predominated. Although
altos are difficult people, if they got their group together, there was
a blending; when this happened there would be harmony in the
world. The heavenly choir evoked such response that the people of
the world began to build bridges, and to reconcile differences. The
alto section brought harmony, and a year of understanding, when
it led the choir.

29

Finally, guess what happened when the sopranos controlled the choir? The high piercing tone of the soprano range penetrated the darkness and jabbed beyond the distant horizon. When the soprano section dominated, it was a year of search and discovery. It was a year of the search for truth.

Each year one section of the heavenly choir took control. It wasn't planned or predicted. It just happened. You could never tell, prior to the event, which would dominate, and which would not. However, the influence of that factor, though subtle, was none-the-less apparent. Think back to the years in past decades and centuries. There were years of strength and faith. There were years of discipline and order. There were years of concord and peace, and there were years of search and discovery. No one knew why, but the answer was obvious to people of faith. *It was the chorus.* It was the angels singing their songs leading up to Christmas and pointing beyond to their influence that lasted throughout the year.

There will be those who doubt what I have said. There always are skeptics, of course. There are people who do not believe in angels. There are people who cannot look at Christmas like they once could when they were young; but none can deny the effect of it all. No one can deny the special feeling that comes at Christmas. Old burdens seem lighter when Christmas rolls around. Old wounds lose a percentage of their potential to bring pain, and despite, the ugliness of life, despite its hardness, people take on almost angelic qualities. And it's no wonder, for some place far beyond what anyone on earth can imagine, there has been a chorus practicing during Advent and performing at Christmas.

One year, several years ago, the unexpected happened, and it led to a catastrophic result. Earth-bound pandemics can happen. Sickness and blizzards, and all manner of sundry means can shut down a choir, and cancel a performance, or diminish the quality of the choral oration. So it was, with the choir in question. One year, several years ago, it happened. Through no fault of anyone, it happened. Certainly, the director was not to blame. The director was the best. The technique had not left him what-so-ever. The choir had a problem. They had been working harder than usual, but things were not going well.

To say the bass section was not strong would be kind. As for the tenor section, for the first time they were sloppy, coming in at the wrong time and never together. They lacked discipline and direction. They were a train wreck or a ship without a rudder. The wheels came off the altos, who were in such an antagonist mood. They sounded more like the rasp of a file grating on the nerves, rather than a harmonious blend. The sopranos pierced the ears with a sound not unlike the howling of a spaniel. Their search was not for truth but for the right note, and most of the time their search was unrewarded.

Insults began to compound the prevailing insanity, and individuals let their feelings get out of control. Accusatory statements were being made, invective and antipathy, and the ushering of discord into the heavenly chorus mounted for the first time. Insults were exchanged. Singers, best of friends, were at each other's throats, acting more like demons than angels, and the crescendo reached its waxing pitch as waxing turned to whining.

The director left the stage in tears as members of the choir stood lost amidst the confusion and turmoil.

Suddenly a voice was heard. It was a voice above the other voices. It was a voice heard many times before, but this time it took on a different pitch. It was THE VOICE OF ALL VOICES (if you know what I mean).

"What's going on here?" THE VOICE asked, "It sounds like the choir is singing off key. It sounds like the choir is disorganized. The choir is acting un-angelic. What's *wrong* with you?"

By now the voices in the choir were worn thin with labor and strain, and the voices of the choir were silent. It was the result of the singing. It was the result of the shouting. THE VOICE continued, "There will be no Christmas chorus this year. There will be no Christmas serenade."

The angels asked each other, "But who will tell the people? Who will convey the message? Who will inspire their hearts with joy?"

THE VOICE paused and said once more, "I have decreed an end to the chorus for this season and for this year."

The angels knew THE VOICE was right. They knew they had ruined Christmas with their bickering and strife.

Well, the Sunday before Christmas came, and the heavens were silenced. The angels milled around at a loss, not knowing what to do or say. The silence was deafening on Earth. The earth people didn't know what the problem was, of course, but they knew something was terribly wrong.

"It doesn't seem like Christmas," they said to one another. The panic of shopping was not accompanied by the spirit that usually infuses the air and people elbowed their way through the merchandise and each other; and even Santa Claus was grumpy. It just didn't seem like Christmas. Old Testament prophesies from yonder years seemed so far away and out of touch. New Testament narratives about Bethlehem seemed like myth or fairy tale, too incredible.

It just didn't seem like Christmas—until something even more unexpected happened. It happened just at midnight on Christmas Eve. It was introduced by the continued silence, followed by the expressions of distress from the people who waited. Just as they began to believe that their deepest fears would be realized that it wouldn't ever seem like Christmas, it happened.

In one hamlet or villa, in a city or borough, or in all of them at the same time—nobody is sure—but it happened. It was the sound of one voice. Some said it was the voice of a child singing. It was a simple song like a child might sing. It was a series of songs you might expect to have heard. Words in songs like, "Jingle bells, jingle all the way," and "Here comes Santa Claus, here comes Santa Claus," and "Silent night, holy night, all is calm, all is bright." A little child may have started it, but the song grew in strength. It probably was a little child who helped people everywhere remember the words and recall the spirit behind those words. Then the whole earth joined in the chorus. People of different faith traditions joined in the spirit of the occasion. There arose from the earth a bass section, singing with such strength that the people knew there were things in which to believe again. There was a tenor section that sang with such discipline that it was reminiscent of the heavenly chorus, and people knew, once more, that the human spirit could be unified. An alto section emerged, to prove that harmonious relationships were not only probable, but also possible to achieve. A soprano section dared to venture to the limit, proving that truth will penetrate the darkness of the deepest ignorance.

The angel chorus was amazed at what was happening. They couldn't believe their ears. In their wildest imagining, it never occurred to them that this could be! Puzzled and confused, and a little bit embarrassed, the angels looked at each other with a vacant, glazed-over expression.

Suddenly, THE VOICE was heard above the angel voices. "Do you hear that?" THE VOICE asked, "Do you hear them down there? They are singing *your* songs. They are praising God and singing, 'Glory to God in the highest, and on earth peace and good will to all people.' Often, we have wondered if they could get the message on their own, and now, we know. This year, and from now on, we will let *them* do the singing. After all, the Word was made flesh and it dwelt among them. We gave them a reason to sing, but they are singing their own song."

This explains why we sing carols at Christmas. We sing them to say to the world, and to the chorus of angels in heaven, that the spirit of the season is not manufactured in plastic, and that the inspiration is not sent down from above. It evolves out of the human experience, as it originally did in Bethlehem. It was a human event. We sing carols to help us remember that Christmas cards and Christmas gifts are extensions of the giver, not the sum of the tag priced in dollars and cents. Choirs sing in churches at Christmas. They lead congregations in worship.

Yet there are some years shrouded in darkness, and the holiday cheer does not make it go away, nor does it help us forget the pain that is in life. People are hurting, and people don't know where to turn, and people are doubtful and filled with fear. It could be it just doesn't seem like Christmas. It reminds you of that one Christmas when the angels didn't sing, and when Christmas almost passed from the scene until the people on earth created their own Christmas.

Any Christmas may be like that unless we join to lift our song. What is needed? What is needed is the songs of Christmas: A serenade to the child.

What is needed is a glimmer of hope, an announcement of joy, a spark of light, a little balance, and a different look. But that's our job.

We believe in the Christmas spirit.

We believe in the season.

We believe in the carols we sing.

We know it is up to us, with God's help, to keep the Spirit of Christmas alive.

Animals in the Story
but not at the Stable

DEER IN THE BACK YARD

TECHNOLOGY IS A WONDERFUL *thing. There are ways we can be in constant contact with each other. Whereas, at one time it was possible to be alone in a crowd, now we can be connected in a crowd even though we are alone, provided we have a cell phone. In former days, Christmas decorations were mostly about color and light, but things have evolved. Now, in addition to color and light, sound is included. . .and robotic movement.*

Years ago, long before televisions had remote or voice control, the most amazing invention was called "The Clapper." As long as devices were plugged in properly, with an almost muted applause, or a soft voice, lights could be commanded to turn on, and televisions could emerge from a state of blankness to the full volume of a quiz show, a situation comedy, or a newscast.

The story I am about to tell is true. It brings together, on a collision trajectory, the Clapper technology and wildlife in the backyard. . .a modern solution that produced an additional problem for an ancient dilemma. What do you do about deer in the backyard when they have overstayed their welcome and have lost their charm? And what does this have to do with Christmas?

When the Magi heard the story, they knew something had happened. In the Christmas story it seems that something always happened when somebody heard something. When the Magi heard about the Christ Child, they sought to find him. When Herod heard about the Child, he sought to determine where the Child was. When Joseph heard the angel, he departed to Egypt. The whole Christmas story involves people hearing, and thus doing, or taking action on what they heard. Hearing came first; doing followed.

One year I received a unique gift for Christmas. I received one of those devices that can turn the TV set off and on with the clap of the hands. I can be in the room, and with a brief sounding of applause, I can turn the TV set on, and with a standing ovation, I can turn it off. It means I can turn off the set late at night without breaking a toe on an improperly placed shoe. It means I can come out from the shower dripping wet, and with the pressing of palms in rapid sequence, I can activate the tube, which will reveal the current status of the Broncos' athletic encounters, at no risk of electrocution.

One week we experienced an infiltration of deer in our back yard. Our neighbor thought it was neat to have Bambi-like critters settling down for the night next to them. It kind of made one feel "out in the wild."

I, too, thought it was neat until I discovered that Bambi likes to eat pine trees. Bambi and his sisters risked life and limb to cross the Turnpike, passing any number of verdant delicacies, in order to chew on the very pine trees I had planted with pick and shovel in my yard. It had been the previous summer when I'd planted them. I remember how difficult that was. My hands bled. My back ached. Those trees I planted provided a hedge wall between ourselves and the good neighbor to the north. "Good fences make good neighbors," Robert Frost had said.

Now they were being reduced to defoliated spikes sticking up from the snow like seven arthritic fingers. We can see every interesting thing our neighbors do in their yard, and all because Bambi and her sisters like to eat my pine trees.

I have tried everything to rid the north 40 of these creatures. I charged them, swinging a baseball bat and using my preacher's voice and words you will not find in the "Sermon on the Mount." I have thrown snowballs and big chunks of ice at their heads. A friend suggested I go to the zoo and get a truck load of lion manure to scare them off. There is something especially problematic with that. It's almost a solution that is as bad as the problem. There is one thing that is effective. The one thing that works, every time, is to take our cocker spaniel, Keefoffer, lift him up to the window, and sing softly into his ear, "Nero, My Dog Has Fleas," (which is to the tune of "Nearer My God to Thee"); he howls, the deer run over to the Presbyterian minister's yard to eat his trees. He lives next door and I suspect he feeds the deer.

There is a problem. I discovered, when Keefoffer howls like that, the TV set comes on or goes off. We can't get him to be quiet. When I sing, the dog hears it, and the dog howls. When the dog howls, the deer hear it, and the deer leave. When the dog howls, and the deer hear it, and the deer leave, then the TV turns on. When the TV turns on, our 10-year-old daughter wakes up, and neither the deer, the dog, the daughter, or her parents can go back to sleep. When it is heard, then it is done.

Well, what did you get for Christmas? What did you get *from* Christmas? What have we heard? What will we do? What will we do because of what we have heard?

Have we made any New Year's resolutions? Are there any resolutions that we make because of what we have heard? If we have heard something, will we be doing something about it?

I resolved to be nicer to my family and to everybody else. I resolved to do that because of what I heard. I heard about a child born in Bethlehem, and it mattered then, and maybe it matters now. I heard that God is not so distant as once I thought God was; now it has become clear there is a new way to be with God, and there is a new way to pray. I heard that love came down at Christmas, and perhaps that is just something people have said in days past, but now it matters because love can turn on lights when the world seems dark.

We have heard. We will do. Christmas makes a difference.

BABY SQUIRREL IN THE STREET
ON CHRISTMAS EVE

No doubt, this reflection sinks to the level of blasphemy since there is a comparison of the Christ Child to a baby squirrel. How absurd! How ridiculous! Who could imagine such a thing?

On the other hand, what will it take to awaken us to the fact that we are each other's keeper, and our lives are spinning out of control? What interruption will help us save ourselves from ourselves? We are so busy taking "selfies" of our journey, we fail to realize the higher road we could take. We are so wrapped up in our Facebook notations, we think community is a friended group, overlooking the fact that human interaction has a tenderness and an embrace that technology cannot replicate. The squirrel on Christmas Eve stopped several people on a busy street at a busy time of year. It stopped me. I will not forget it. . .

The town where I live is not an unfriendly town, but it is "a-friendly." People will help you if you can stop them long enough, but when you walk toward them, they will not look at you, nor will they speak to you. The exception is at a liquor store. Applejack Liquor is the friendliest place in the village, and the most crowded. What does that say about a town, when the most jovial people are the ones searching the shelves for the purpose of purchasing additional inebriants? In a season of light and joy, in a time of lists and tasks, in a time of parties and people coming together, there still seems to be the need to dull the pain with spirits, and to lift the mood in an artificial and unhealthy way. . .

It was Christmas Eve and I was driving into the town. I was on one final shopping trip. The cars coming east and west were stopped, for no apparent reason. On closer inspection, it was revealed there was a baby squirrel on a busy street moving in circles, looking confused and upset. He did not know which way to run. There was a lot of traffic and the cars were not moving. Every car stopped for the baby squirrel, but how would this be resolved?

A young woman was walking on the sidewalk on the north side of the street, and she saw the dilemma. She waved to us, and we were all thankful for her intervention. She tried to get the squirrel to move out of the middle of the street, but it kept running in circles. Finally, she took her foot and gently shoved the animal up in the air and it ran back. She took her foot again and lifted the animal closer to the side of the road. The squirrel ran off and the motorists applauded this young woman who had come to the rescue.

There is a Christmas message in this somewhere. Christmas is a time when God saw the people of the world moving rapidly on their way, and God put the baby into the middle of the road; the people stopped, and some were inspired to perform acts of kindness. Of course, most people failed to notice at the time, and if they had noticed, they would not have imagined it. The idea of the presence of God in the form of a baby, born in such unremarkable circumstances, might be considered unlikely. In fact, that is *precisely* how it came about. A child was born. Every year we stop what we are doing, and where we are going, and we notice. It is the way God gets our attention. It's God's interruption.

Baby Noises on Christmas Eve

ANYONE WHO HAS BEEN given the awesome responsibility of developing and leading a worship service understands what an honor it is. Great effort is given to make certain there is a level of excellence that enables the congregation to tap into the spiritual power that comes when God is worshipped, human issues are addressed, and hope is discovered.

When it comes to worship in the Christmas season, the imperative to make worship the best it can be is elevated. Sometimes, Christmas Eve is the only experience some people have of the church.

Worship of God, in a church sanctuary, is important. When the words that are spoken, the music that is sung, and the liturgy that is read connects with the people who are present, lives can be changed. The Christmas Eve service is one of the most important hours of worship in the life of the church. As a minister, preacher, and pastor, I did everything I could do to make it the best it could be. Sometimes, I failed. One of those times involved prerecorded baby noises:

There was a couple in the church who had been waiting to adopt a baby for years. Three weeks before Christmas they were told to prepare. They had been approved to adopt. They were told their baby would arrive very soon. They were to receive a little girl who had been born recently, and the mother had agreed to relinquish her for adoption.

Jack and Kathy were so excited to hear the news. They came to the church to tell me and the other staff members in the office. They were going to be parents! They had thought they were too old to be allowed to adopt, so this was like a dream coming true.

Within the following week it happened. Their daughter arrived and Jack and Kathy brought her home. They were so happy. They invited me to meet their newborn daughter. She was a beautiful child, and they were a picture-perfect family. While I was in their home, I had an idea. Sometimes, good ideas happen on the spur of a moment and you must act on them.

Christmas is about the birth of a baby. Jack and Kathy were parents of a newborn child. I pondered the possibility of bringing the two happenings together. If we had decided to reenact the Manger Scene, I might have suggested we place the baby in the manger for the Service. If the Christmas Eve services had been scheduled to begin at the end of the afternoon, I might have thought we could introduce the baby to the congregation, and there might have been a baptism. The first service on Christmas Eve began at 7 and the last service began at 11. Having a baby involved in something at those hours was unthinkable.

Then I thought about "baby noises." I asked Jack and Kathy if they would take a tape recorder and record some of their baby's noises. I told them I wanted to have the congregation hear the sweet sounds of a baby on Christmas Eve. In my mind, there were some similarities between the expectation of the mother and father who had waited so long for the arrival of their adopted child, and the birth of the Christ Child and the expectant feelings attributed to the Word of God becoming flesh. It seemed appropriate for those of us who were celebrating the birth of the Christ Child to hear the sounds of a baby. It seemed like such a good idea.

As the days moved ever so quickly toward Christmas, I did not hear from Kathy and Jack. Since I had not received the tape by a week before Christmas, I assumed they were not able to accomplish the task and I gave up on my idea of having recorded baby sounds for the Christmas Eve service.

They arrived for the 7 o'clock service beaming with joy, with little Deborah in their arms. Much to my surprise they handed me the tape. I had a brief time to carry out the plan. Hastily, I ran up the steps and gave the tape to the sound technician and asked him to play it during the silent prayer. Due to the late arrival of the recording, I was the only one who knew about this venture in sight and sound. I imagined the quiet cooing of a baby. I thought of the gentle breathing sounds a baby makes, and how this would add so much to our celebration of the birth of the Christ Child. I thought of the Christmas Carol, "Away in a Manger." The words of that song inspired this experiment. The song reminds us, "Away in a manger, no crib for a bed, the little Lord Jesus lay down his sweet head." It goes on to say, "The cattle are lowing, the baby awakes, the little Lord Jesus, no crying he makes."

It seemed a perfect match. It brought together the young couple and their new-born child and the Nativity scene that everyone in that Sanctuary would be able to imagine on that Christmas Eve, enhanced by the soft sound of a baby. What I had forgotten, and what I really should have remembered, is that babies do not usually make quiet sounds. Cooing is punctuated by other noises that are much less given to holy worship of God. Having called for the silent prayer and standing in the pulpit, prepared to be hearing sweet baby noises, it was evident from the start that this may not have been a good idea. The noises were loud, and strident, and strange. People jerked up from their meditative posture. The baby's belching noises brought about a recoiled antiphonal response from the congregated, and before that silent prayer was over, I thought the Candle Lighting Service had been ruined. Some people thought there was a problem with the pipe organ, and a repair person should be summoned. Other people thought there was a protest group trying to disrupt the service. Most people were confused. Many were concerned.

However, Jack and Kathy were proud of the involvement of their daughter on her first Christmas Eve. I pondered what it all meant.

There were other problems in the service. The choir was so shaken by the frightening baby noises, and their that anthem was so off key, they had to start it over. The ushers could not find the extra candles, and there was a section of the congregation that went without light. One of the acolytes fell asleep and he began snoring. It was the worst Christmas Eve service I had been party to, and I was embarrassed. The organist threatened to resign, and the choir director had a migraine headache. Certainly, most of the people did not leave the service with the Christmas spirit. Nor did I leave with the Christmas spirit. That happened twenty-five years ago, and the feeling of despair remains with me whenever I think of that December 24th debacle. In fact, I refer to that event as the "Screaming Baby" service. Little did I know there had been a dog in the balcony that night as well. We'd had the potential of baby noises and a barking dog.

In the back of my mind I recalled that there may have been a dog in the balcony, but that did not occupy much of my attention. It was a mystery, but a faint memory of a bad night. There could have been a dog in the balcony, but it did beg the question, "Why was there a dog in the balcony?"

It was not until a year later that I received a letter that helped clear up this mystery. The letter was from a young woman who wanted to let us know how much that Christmas Eve worship service had meant to her. She wrote that she had been living on the street. She was homeless and without a friend except for her German Shepherd dog, who went everywhere she went. She had run away from home and she was very confused and lost when she came to the church on Christmas Eve.

The 7 o'clock Service was about to begin when she came into the church. The Sanctuary was almost full, and she had received rejection in a variety of ways that night. Storeowners and restaurant owners in a hurry to get home to their families did not have time to help, or even notice, this runaway girl and her dog. She was homesick and lonely, and needed to find some encouragement and some hope. Thoughts of ending her life had entered her mind.

The ushers were in the back of the Sanctuary passing out bulletins. It is not certain which usher it was who dealt with her and her dog that night. Several of them remember that it happened but none of them will take credit for what they did. What they did was to offer her hospitality. They invited her into our church. They suggested she was welcome to be there, and they were pleased she had come. As for the dog, they suggested she and her dog walk up the steps into the balcony. They made some mention of how a barking dog in the middle of the Candle Lighting Service would lend a special touch to the occasion of welcoming the Christ Child into the world. After all, in the story, it is assumed that there were sheep and cattle; and who is to say there wasn't a stray dog in the barn in back of the crowded inn? She assured the ushers that her dog would not be disruptive. She and her dog headed for the balcony.

At the end of the service, one of the ushers saw them leaving the Sanctuary. He walked over to her, and he shook her hand warmly. In that handshake was a fifty-dollar bill. According to her letter, this Christmas Eve worship service was a turning point for this young woman.

The night we had baby noises, also we had a dog in the balcony. The mystery was solved. At the Christmas Eve Service in which everything went wrong, one thing went right. This young woman claimed, because of the kindness of our people, and the hospitality she was shown, she was able to put some things together. Her life began to take shape, and she found hope, and a reason to live. She began to act on her future instead of waiting for the future to come to her. She came to the church that had baby noises during the service. . .Christmas Eve, in the balcony of the church, there was hope, and she had caught a glimpse of it.

Our ushers and our church had helped her turn her life around. We made a difference to one human being who might make a difference to others. You never know. We never will know where it stops, but we do have some idea where it starts. It starts with treating people with dignity and respect, and finding some way to believe in them, even when they have trouble believing in themselves. Opportunities present themselves every day, and you never know what can happen, or where they will lead.

The letter from this young woman was postmarked, "Connecticut." The letter came from New Haven, Yale Divinity School. A young woman who found home in a church on Christmas Eve, when she felt alone and unwelcomed, had decided to work in the church, dedicating herself to welcoming strangers who come in the night.

It was not the sermon I preached, but it might have been the candles that were lighting the darkness. It was not the choir that fumbled the anthem, but it might have been what they sang after their restart. Maybe it was a combination of things: the friendliness of the greeting, the generosity of the man who gave her the fifty-dollar bill, the softness of the carols, and even the baby noises during the silent prayer. In a worship service when nothing seemed to go right, a most important thing was almost perfect. The message of Christmas, of love, of hope, of joy, and peace, comes through, in spite of us.

Following in My Father's Footsteps

I SUPPOSE IT IS *true for everyone, at least it's this way for me. My father died when I was nine years old. I have memories of him, and there are ways he influenced me. He was a talented and creative man. He left me two gifts. I have the roll-top desk he built, and I have a pair of his shoes. I use the desk to do all my writing, but I doubted it would be possible to wear his shoes. My foot is a size 13. And his shoes are sized 12. However, I just knew there was some way I could fit my foot into the smaller space.*

One year on Christmas Eve, I decided to wear my father's shoes; I wanted to honor him and to experience his presence as I conducted the services that evening. I managed to wedge my feet into the shoes. It was possible but it was not easy.

In some way the decision was not a good one. However, circumstances produced an interesting result that became a tradition. Some stories are best told poetically. Every Christmas Eve, until the shoes wore out, I followed in my father's footsteps.

Christmas is a special time in the life of many folk,
But when you work within a church it can be such a joke.
To celebrate the birth of Jesus, almost everyone will know,
There is so much tradition, and there is a kind of flow.
Candles are to be lighted, and held in every hand,
While singing "Silent Night," which the fire codes have banned.
Preachers lose their pulpits if this evening is not right,
Congregants stand ready for a tradition-judging fight.

Sometimes lights are lowered before the fire is ever spread,
Sometimes flames get too close to another person's head.
Sometimes lights are left on high and the flame is nullified,
And the people stand impatient and the look ain't deified.
Preachers pack their books when Christmas Eve has gone awry,
Nobody really cares to learn the reason why.
It could have been the fool who turned the lights on way too late,
Or the secretary who ordered candles after the expiration date.
It could have been the choir that missed the cue
they should have got,
And sang the anthem poorly, in an unanticipated spot.
When tradition called for silence,
there was a loud and strident sound,
And the congregation was perplexed,
and everybody looked around.
You try to get it right, on the night of the Savior's birth,
There is nothing more important in heaven or on earth.
I always worried about the fire, and the danger in the night,
And the proximity of the candles to the person on the right.
Or the one whose longish locks hung in front of the one behind,
I always tried to give instruction, and always to remind.
And I kept a water bucket in the pulpit, just in case
There was a fire in the building, with no time, alas, to waste.
But on this one Christmas, I decided I would dare,
To walk in my father's footsteps, and his shoes I chose to wear.
My Dad and I were never close, he died when I was nine,
But he bought only the best, and his shoes were very fine.
They were a little snug, for his foot was not so large,
And my foot was extra big, like a river toting barge.
When the service augured down into "Silent Night" that year,
And the candles lit the room, and my heart was filled with fear,
And the bucket full of water in the pulpit I had set,
Without thinking or looking down, fate and I had met.
I stepped into the bucket, and the water soaked my shoe,
And the only hope I had was that maybe no one knew.
But the leather foot apparel, took an unexpected turn,
For every step henceforth led the people to discern.

The syncopated rhythm of the squish of leather wet,
In the "Silent Nighted" singing, was the best and ever yet.
Tradition called for replication, and every year on that special night,
The preacher was told to wear a wet shoe to accentuate delight.
I followed in my father's footsteps,
though I think he would be proud,
To know it was his noisy shoes that pleased the Christmas crowd.

REFLECTION

There is a rhythm to Christmas. It is heard in the story, in the music, and in the preparation that leads to Christmas Day. Children hear it best, but the rhythm is heard by everyone who is captured by the meaning of the Christmas Story. Some suggest Santa Claus is ancillary to the story, but I do not believe that. Some believe there is something wrong with the merchandising of Christmas, and there is more bling and buzz than there should be. But people are in a giving mood, and what better could there be than for a focus shift from ourselves to others? If seeking to find something someone else might like to have, in the name of Christmas as the motivation, that cannot be all wrong.

The rhythm is in the heartbeat of the believer, in the cadence of the carols, in the blinking of the lights, and in the sparkle in the eyes, as the candles flicker in the darkness. For me, the rhythm was in the shoes that squeaked a beat as I walked up the aisle while the congregation sang. My father walked with me that night, and every year after that first time that I walked in my father's shoes.

Coincidence or a Nod from God?

SOME THINGS IN LIFE cannot be explained. The Church has offered the story that a virgin can give birth. The Christmas narrative is not just about a birth, it's about the discovery of a miracle. Christmas is about looking at the impossible as thinkable. Christmas is about experiencing the unbelievable and beginning to cast out doubt. I do not know if angels can sing in the night, I've never heard them. Nor do I know if stars can lead Magi to an obscure Inn in the middle of a busy town. However, I do know there are some things that cannot be explained.

There is much in our lives that could be called coincidence. Coincidence is the confluence of factors that occur when a problem has a solution, and the solution to the problem comes in unexpected ways. Coincidence is the merging of a thought with the source of the thought. For example, you happen to be thinking about someone you have not seen or heard from for months, and that person calls you that same day or even within the same hour. Coincidence is a "God Nod." It is the intersection of natural law with an unnatural or unexpected consequence, reminding us of the supernatural. It shakes our confidence and reminds us that we do not have all the answers. It awakens us to the realities beyond our knowing. It affirms our faith, and yet, it shakes up our basic convictions. It encourages our boldness, and yet, it promotes humility. It inspires us to risk, and yet, makes us realize our timidity. The following stories are of minor importance and yet, looking for the incidence of coincidence every day can be of major consequence. Since the way we look determines what we can see, when we understand the importance of coincidence, there is much more that comes into our view. With eyes able to see it, we can experience a Nod from God.

THE WRONG WORDS WERE RIGHT

This ad appeared in a local newspaper: "Tombstone for sale. Especially appropriate for a person named McCormack." What are the chances someone named McCormack might be reading that newspaper and thinking about dying and needing a tombstone?

A similar, remarkable event happened to me at Christmas. It involved the gift of a shirt and the name on the shirt and the person who received the shirt. It was two weeks before Christmas and I decided to order a gift for a friend whose husband had recently died. I thought it might bring Janet some joy if she were to have a shirt I had seen in a catalogue. It was a blue, short-sleeve shirt, and it had sequined letters that read, "My favorite people call me 'Grammy.'" She was the proud grandmother of four young grandchildren, and they all called her "Grammy." It seemed a perfect gift. Often, people who are grieving the death of a loved one have an especially difficult time at Christmas. This gift would remind her of those she loved and that she is loved. That is a good thing to remember when one is sad—especially at Christmas.

The shirt arrived on December 22nd , so the timing was perfect. Sometimes you try to do something nice for someone and it gives more pleasure to you, the giver, than you would have imagined. In this case, I felt very pleased as I pondered the gift and the recipient.

Sometimes, however, the gift does not live up to the expectations that inspired its purchase. That was true in this case. My Christmas spirit was diminished when I opened the box. The shirt was the right color. It was the right size, and it had the sequined lettering. Sadly, the message on the shirt was not what was expected or hoped for. Instead of proclaiming, "My favorite people call me 'Grammy.'" it read, "My favorite people call me 'Gigi.'"

How could this happen? Who is named "Gigi?" I did not know anyone who is called "Gigi." Gigi is a name you give a dog or a hamster. What will I do with a shirt that does not fit me, that has a name that does not fit anyone? How could this have happened? Why did it happen? What will I do? What could I do to redeem this screw up? Had I misread the ad? Had I clicked on the wrong box? Had the mail order company made the mistake? There was no time to send for another shirt because my friend would be leaving town the day after Christmas.

Our next-door neighbor's name is Genca. She is a wonderful person and a good friend, but Genca is an odd name. I never met a person named Genca. I don't know why she is named Genca. I think it's a family name, given to her when she was a child. Maybe it was an expression she had when she was learning to talk. Genca has grandchildren. I wondered what her grandchildren called her. Was it possible that someone whose name was Genca might be called Gigi by her grandchildren? What are the chances that could happen? It occurred to me to ask the question, but it seemed remote and unlikely a woman who lived next door might have the same nickname printed on the shirt that came with the wrong name.

However, I've learned over the years that Christmas does produce unlikely coincidence. After all, the Christmas story is about one woman who gave birth to a baby and she thought she was too old, and another woman who gave birth to a baby and she thought she was too young. Both Elizabeth and Mary asked the question, "What are the chances this could happen?" Things like this happen at Christmas.

With the misnamed shirt in my hands, I called my neighbor.

"Genca," I said, "Does anyone in your family call you Gigi?"

She answered, "Yes, my grandchildren and my children call me Gigi."

I said, "Can you meet me at your front door?"

I delivered the shirt meant for Janet, and gave it to a woman named Genca, whose children and grandchildren called her Gigi. She wanted to pay me for the shirt, but I declined remuneration. I was happy to unload the shirt I had ordered by mistake. It would have been a difficult purchase to explain.

What can be concluded from this? Obviously, one needs to be more careful before placing an order via internet. Clearly, if one is to give a surprise gift, it is best not to announce it in advance. I am still looking for something for Janet. But there is a much more important conclusion, and it has to do with the spirit of giving and the way in which an effort to do something nice for someone has a ripple effect. The right gift goes to the right person if one is willing to be open to seeing it. Things have a way of working out, even when it seems there is no way—like when there is no room in the Inn, but still a child is born in the middle of the night, and a star shines brightly overhead.

Whatever can be said about Christmas, it is a time when people try to do something for each other. Some speak of the Christ Child as "One of God's Gifts to the World." I call it a "Nod from God," reminding us an important part of our time on Earth must be spent giving back because we have graciously been given so much.

The Broken Light Turned On

DAVID, WHO TOLD ME *this story, is completely credible. I believe he believes it. I can't explain it. Neither can he, but it is one of the most incredible stories.*

Grief is a burden. Our loved ones die and we wonder if our lives are fit to inherit the legacy they left for us. The ideals they lived by inspire us. Their examples motivate us. Their ideas reside with us and, at times, we find ourselves expressing some of the same values they taught us. It's almost as if they are living through us. It's almost as if their voices are voices we can hear, and their encouragement is something we can feel.

I don't know about life after death. I don't understand the life after this life, and I'm not sure there is one. I doubt there is a Hell. I can't imagine the concept of eternal punishment being inflicted upon us because of the mistakes we have made, the sins we have committed, or the crimes we were able to commit without punishment. I do think the essential influence others have had upon our lives continues to leave a lasting impression. I do think the dead have not died in vain.

This story is about such an impression. The influence of a man transcended his death and was conveyed through music. The details of this story are open for debate. However, the influence of the "Music Man" cannot be discounted.

David is a good friend and he is a truthful man. I have known him a long, long time. He isn't inclined to make things up or try to put a spin on things that challenge the way things really are. He told me the facts. I believe him.

His father died in the summer of the year. David admired his father and his father's death was understandably difficult. His father was a music teacher in a Kansas high school.

Before his father took over the music program in that small high school, there was not much of an outlet for the students. His father established a marching band that competed in the state competitions. Not only did the music program inspire the teenagers who participated, it became a source of pride for the entire town. In fact, one year the marching band won the Kansas state competition, and his father became a celebrity in the town. They called him, "The Music Man."

On Christmas, following David's father's death, his mother, his sisters and their husbands and their children all came to David's house for the holiday. David had a small house and, with so many people visiting, David had to sleep on the living room couch. Beside the couch there was a broken lamp that had not been operable for some time. It wouldn't turn on. David assumed there was a loose wire or some problem with the switch, but he had not had a chance to have it repaired.

In the middle of the night on Christmas Eve, the year his father died, the lamp turned on. David was surprised. That lamp hadn't worked for months, but there was no question about it, the lamp had turned on in the middle of the night. It was strange.

David said out loud, "I hear you, Dad." He laughed at himself as he said those words. To his shock and amazement, after he had spoken, the lamp turned off. He began to think his father was sending a message, although he doubted it. Surely, it was a coincidental happening. For all he knew, that lamp might have been turning off and on in the middle of the night every night.

David told his family about the lamp that next morning. He told them the lamp that did not work had turned on. He told them when he spoke to his father, it turned off. He showed them how the lamp did not work. He could tell they doubted his story. Who would believe that a lamp that did not work, would work, and then, when spoken to, would turn off? It was too strange to be believed!

On Christmas Day, after the family had opened their presents and finished their meal, David's mother said, "Why don't we sing some Christmas Carols?"

The family gathered around the piano, and while David played, they began to sing Carols. David said, "Let's sing 'Silent Night.' Dad loved that song." It was true and everyone knew it. David's father loved "Silent Night." In fact, he had written a version of the Carol that the high school orchestra played at their winter concert.

Tears came to the eyes of many members of the family as they began singing "Silent Night," and memories flooded their minds. Suddenly, the lamp that did not work turned on.

Let me repeat that. In the middle of the day, on Christmas Day, a family, standing around a piano began singing "Silent Night," thinking of a man whose life was music. Then it happened; the lamp, the one that did not work, turned on. They stopped singing, and the lamp turned off. They stood there in the silence and looked at one another.

David told me this story several years ago. He calls this story, "Someone's Messing with the Light." When David remembers this event and tells of it, he adds these words, "I don't understand this. I do not explain how it happened. I just tell you what happened." Then David says, "Maybe, on some level, there is life after we die."

I believe David's story. I call this a "Nod from God," reminding us that the influence of our loved ones lives in our hearts and minds long after they're gone.

The Nicest Man in Town

CHRISTMAS GIFT-GIVING IS A *challenge for me. I struggle with two conflicting values when it comes to shopping for the people I know and love. I want to give a gift to the person wants to receive, but there are gifts people do not know they want to receive and are surprised when they receive them from me. Sometimes they are disappointed. There is a tension with gift-giving, between the value of appropriateness and the value of surprise.*

The following story is not about the search for the right gift. It's about the discovery of an amazing man who crafted the gift I happened to give.

A few days before Christmas I was in a store looking for a gift that might be a surprise for my sister. I wanted to find something she would like to have, but something that she would never buy for herself. I wanted to find something useful, but not too pragmatic. I visited a rather eclectic store that sold novelty items such as paintings of dogs, geodes the size of tabletops, recipe boxes lined in felt, and wood carvings. I was drawn to a wood carving cut-out that depicted the Nativity Scene. It came flat in a box, but it could be telescoped open when set on a table to be three dimensional. It seemed the perfect gift for my sister, and, as it turned out, it was.

The woman who sold it to me said, "This was made by someone who lives in Fort Collins. I know him. He is the nicest man in town. His name is Dean and he is a college professor."

Then there was a nod from God. I took my gift home and showed it to my wife. I told her the woman who sold it to me told me she knew the man who made it, and she said his name was Dean Miller, and that she had said he was the nicest man in town.

My wife said, "I think I know him, too. I worked on a city committee with him. I think I would like one of those wood carvings as well."

I returned to the store and purchased the last wood carving made by the nicest man in town for my wife.

On Christmas Eve I took our wood carving to the church and used it as an illustration in the sermon. I recall standing up in the pulpit and delivering my sermon, and saying to the congregation, "I want to show you this wood carving I bought. You see how it telescopes open. If you look at the pieces of this wood carving, you can really tell the story with each piece. You can telescope Mary out and emphasize her. You can telescope Joseph out of the wood block and that showcases him. Most importantly, you can telescope the baby Jesus out of the wood block and focus on that part of the story, You can see the star above Mary and Joseph and the baby Jesus."

Then I said to the congregation, "What makes this even more special is the fact that this was crafted by a man, described by the person who sold it to me as, 'the nicest man in town.' His name is Dean Miller, and he teaches at the University. Wouldn't that be something to be known as the nicest man or the nicest woman or the nicest child in town?"

There was some commotion in the congregation when I said *that*. Now, the Sanctuary holds 1,000 people and it was filled, but someone in the congregation attending the service was trying to get my attention. In the middle of my sermon on Christmas Eve, someone was trying to get me to stop speaking. They wanted to tell me something. It must have been important. That kind of thing does not happen in our United Methodist Churches. It was very unusual.

In the front of the sanctuary, a man said, in a voice that many could hear, "You're talking about Dean Miller, the nicest man in town. Dean and Donna Miller are sitting here in the Sanctuary."

Dean and Donna Miller had never been in that church before that night and it was that night I chose to use Dean's wood carving as the basis for my sermon. I had no idea he would be there. He had no idea I would be speaking of him. How does that happen? This is one of those mysteries that has no explanation. I cannot explain it, but I tell you it is true. It happened. Was it just a coincidence? Maybe! Perhaps it was another example of a "Nod from God."

Epilogue

IN THE "MEMORY CARE" section of a nursing home, a woman, who has lost most of her cognitive ability, wanders the halls. It is the darkest time of year. It is, in fact, Christmas Eve, and her name is Alice. If she were to be asked, she could not tell you her name. She cannot speak. Macular degeneration has taken much of the sharpness out of her vision. She sees forms and structures, but cannot distinguish the substance of what she is seeing.

The staff call Alice "The Walker." They say she walks the halls day and night. What is the reason for this behavior? Why does she walk? Is she trying to stay fit? Does she think she is on a mission. . .or a pilgrimage? Does the walking allow her to find herself? Most often, when she walks her pace is rapid and the other residents must watch out that she doesn't walk into them or over them. There is a frenzied quality to her walking. It's as if there is an importance to the destination, and yet, the expression on her face reflects contorted pain, almost panic. She is going nowhere and is in a hurry to get there.

This night is different. It is Christmas Eve and her gait is slow. That is unusual. One other thing is different. This night she is carrying something. Alice has something in her arms. She smiles and lifts her hands to reveal the object she is carrying. It is a plastic baby doll. There is a beautiful smile on Alice's face. On Christmas Eve, this confused and agitated woman is calmed by carrying a baby doll.

One of the nurses identified the reason for the slower pace, the smile on her face, and the uncharacteristically calm disposition. The nurse said of Alice, "It seems to me, on Christmas Eve, she is carried by the baby in her arms."

For each of us, young or old, rich or poor, believer or doubter, Christian or non-Christian, when we come to understand the deeper joy of Christmas and the universal message of hope that it conveys, we too, are carried by the baby in our hearts.

Many people in the darkest time of their lives are carried by the baby: the Christ Child. This is the reason we listen to the Christmas Carols on our car radios, I-Pods, and other devices. That is what I did after September 11, 2001. In the middle of September, decades ago, I needed to experience the comfort of the soft music, and the idea that God was here with us, as we watched and experienced that horrific series of events.

The interpretations of the Christmas story are widespread. Scholars generally debunk the details. They suggest the birth of Jesus could not have happened as Matthew and Luke have written it. There is no record of a Census, so no need to make a pilgrimage to Bethlehem. There is no evidence of the slaughter of children, so no need for Mary and Joseph to flee to Egypt. There is no documentation of a star leading shepherds to the Inn; had there been shepherds in the field, it would not have been in December, but rather in the Spring of the year.

Other believers develop alternative viewpoints seeking to prove that the Biblical texts are "literally" true. The confluence of two planets could explain the star in the sky. The Census might have happened because there is some evidence of a Census occurring at a different time. As for other miraculous aspects of the story, such as the idea of a virgin giving birth, some will offer a refrain that says, "With God, all things are possible."

I think, it is the uncertainty of the story, and the dubiousness of the elements in the Christmas narrative, that give it the deeper meaning. The fact that it can't be explained is the most powerful element. In other words, the obscurity of the birth of Jesus gives us a glimpse of what it means to experience "God with us."

Epilogue

The ultimate point of the Incarnation is not just about God appearing in the form of a baby in a manger, in a town in which there was no room, and through a story that cannot be completely understood. The contradictions, confusion, and lack of clarity about Jesus' birth are precisely an invitation for us to look for evidence of "God with us" in the contradictions, confusion, and un-clarity of our lives. The stories contained in this book point to other times that are equally disturbing.

When death comes, we look for meaning amid our sorrow. When disappointment takes away our hope, we look for a glimmer of possibility upon which a new dream can begin to grow. When failure to live up to our expectations build, in us, a sense of guilt, we seek to find a way to turn our lives around so that there will be another time and we will do better.

I have tried to point to the presence of the Holy, and the expression of the sacred in unlikely places. It came in a nursing home to a cranky old lady, to a young couple dealing with the death of their four-year-old daughter, to a school principal in a blizzard on the day before Christmas break, to a shepherd girl who kept a secret, to a town that was stopped in its fast pace by a squirrel on a busy street, and to a family experiencing a flickering light on a broken lamp.

My intention in writing this book is to suggest that the Christmas story is what Paul Tillich called, "The Eternal Now." Some truth is so profound it cannot be expressed in words, because it is contained in a story that cannot be grasped by the mind without being advised by the heart. Miracles are not the suspension of nature, but the fulfillment of it, and the most important part of a story is the meaning the story conveys.

Christmas is a great example of the depth of the Christian faith, but there is a part of its meaning that is contained in almost all faith traditions. The story, and the message it carries, can be understood on so many levels. It brings the idea of God from the supernatural belief in a power over and beyond us, to a sense that the God we worship is the supportive presence we experience in the high points and low points of our search for meaning. God is as much within us as God is beyond us.

In my 43 years of preaching about the Christmas story, this is what I have discovered:

1. The most important parts of Christmas are the least obvious.
2. There is a universal aspect to the story that transcends Christianity.
3. The inexplicable is best left unexplained. There is mystery in life. The Christmas story highlights the importance of mystery.
4. Ultimately, Christmas gives us hope that things can be better; that we can become better people; that peace can come on Earth; and that there is poetry in life, even when there is inequity and injustice.

God with us, Immanuel, is not just a theological premise, but, as communicated in the mystery of the story of the birth of Jesus, is a promise. The promise is discovered in those everyday moments when God surprises us in ways we could not anticipate, in stories we cannot explain, and in places we would never expect—like Bethlehem.

Made in the USA
Las Vegas, NV
03 November 2021

33594751R00042